AF488395

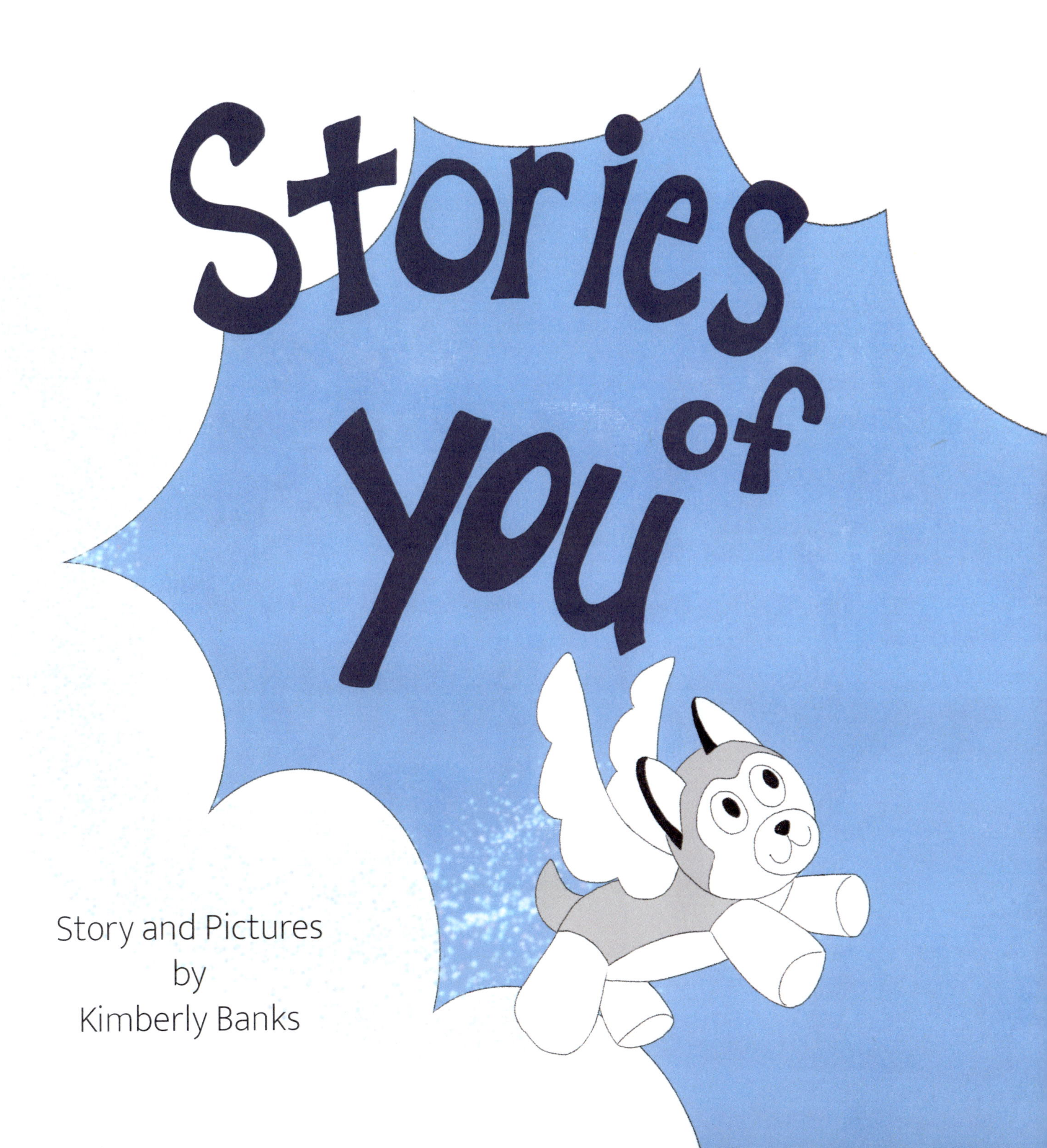

Stories of You
Story and Pictures
by
Kimberly Banks

To those who fight, to those who love them, and to our treasures in Heaven.

For Mom…
"…being confident of this, that he who began a good work in you will carry it on to completion
until the day of Christ Jesus." Philippians 1:6

To my children…
You will seek me and find me when you seek me with all your heart. Jeremiah 29:4

Special thanks to Sean…
For always encouraging me.

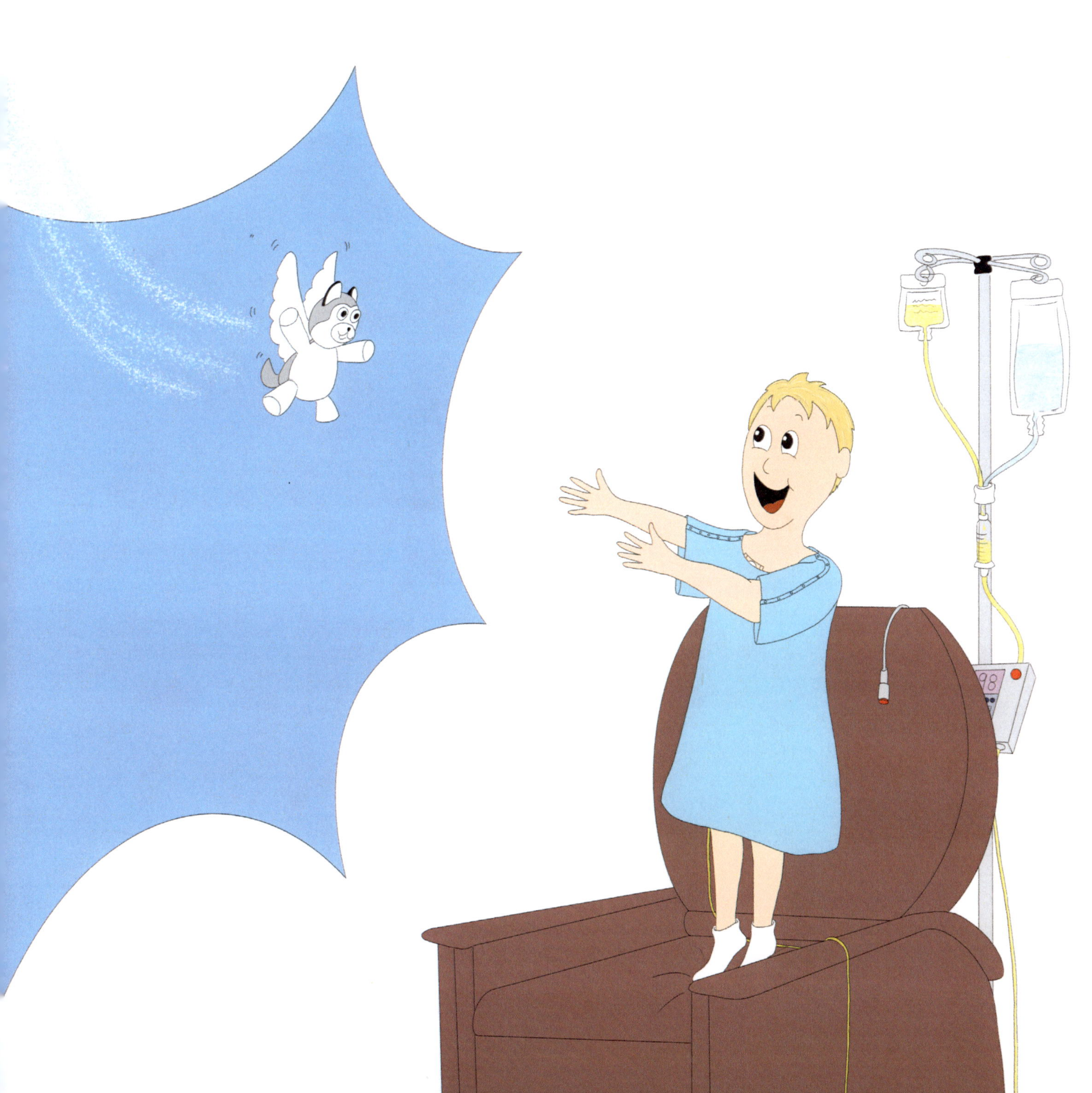

Momma tells me stories of you,
sometimes late at night,

When I've had a bad, bad dream
to help me feel alright.

Sometimes,
when we're playing games
and feeling silly too,

She tells me
of your laughter and the joy
that came from you.

John
3:17

Sometimes, on a Sunday morning
standing in a pew,
She tells me
that you used to
love to
sing and worship
too.

Sometimes, on an ocean trip when the sun is still asleep,

We search for shells
just like you did,
that Momma lets me
keep.

Sometimes, in the Spring
when the lilac and iris bloom,

We pick their flowers fresh for you and
smell their sweet perfume.

Sometimes, when the days are hot and full of summer sun,

We play like you did in the lake to try and have some fun.

But...lately I've been feeling sick, and scared and anxious too.
The truth is, I have cancer. Momma says you had it too.

Momma says you held
me once when I was just
two weeks,

You whispered softly, sweet baby,
and kissed my nose and cheeks.

Exodus 14:14

Momma said you were so sick, but God knew what to do.
He took you home to live with Him high up above the blue.
He welcomed you with open arms,
and angels singing there.
And I'm so thankful for that place of love
he made to share.

1 corinthians 2:9

Cancer's really hard sometimes and makes me feel so small,
But Momma says you told her God loves us through it all.

So, when all the needles
come and scare me
everyday, she tells me
we should pray for God
to take the fear away.

I think God let's you see me
and help me when you can.

I think He gives you jobs
up there to help
His great big plan.

Jeremiah 29:11-13

So, Grandma, if you hear me, please say a prayer for me,
Ask God to take this cancer and help me to be free.

This cancer makes me very tired, and sad and worried too.
My blood is sick and needs some help to make it
good as new.

So sometimes, when I'm anxious about things still yet to come,
Momma says you told her to live each day one by one.
And sometimes,
when the fevers start, and I'm cold and shaking too,
We snuggle underneath the quilts of love made just by you.

I love you
Bright Be Thy Dreams
Phillippians 4:6-7
TRUTH the Life
Jesus
Sweet Dreams
you will always be my sunshine
Love Mom

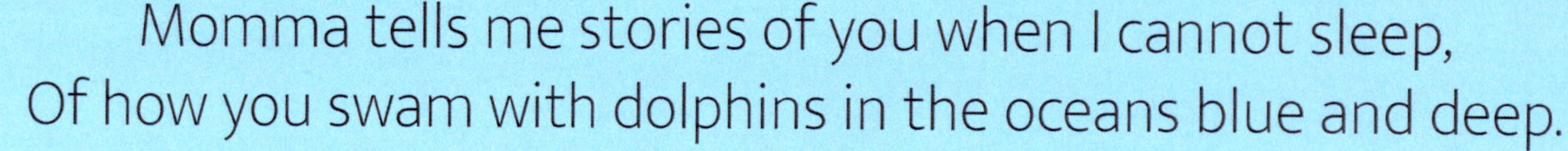

Momma tells me stories of you when I cannot sleep,
Of how you swam with dolphins in the oceans blue and deep.

2 Corinthians 11:5

Or how you traveled to distant lands. You went so far away, to give your love to someone else who needed brighter days.

And then when you
were very sick, for
others you would pray.
Because you wanted
them to know that
Jesus is the way.

What I love the best about Momma's stories of you,
Is how they bring me closer to the
grandma I wish I knew.

Momma says you fought so hard,
now I must fight hard too.
Cancer's something that we share,
I wish it wasn't true.

But we also share a God who loves,
and heals and saves us too.
No More Chemo!
END OF TREATMENT
But thanks be to God! He gives us the VICTORY through our Lord Jesus Christ.
1 Corinthians 15:57

And I just can't wait to meet you,
in Heaven high above.

Where we will be together
surrounded in
God's love.

But Momma says I can't go yet, I have too much to do.
So, I will stay with Momma while God allows me to.

PROVERBS 3:5-6
And someday when I'm all grown up
and lived my whole life through,

I'll share God's love by telling my stories,
like Momma did for you.